The Blooming Void

Peter C. Fernbach

BlazeVOX [books]

Buffalo, New York

The Blooming Void by Peter C. Fernbach

Copyright © 2010

Published by BlazeVOX [books]

Printed in the United States of America

Book design by Geoffrey Gatza

First Edition
ISBN: 9781935402916
Library of Congress Control Number 2009941032

BlazeVOX [books]
303 Bedford Ave
Buffalo, NY 14216

Editor@blazevox.org

publisher of weird little books

BlazeVOX [books]

blazevox.org

2   4   6   8   0   9   7   5   3   1

B   X

Acknowledgments

"We Read with a Difference", "Difference of Opinion: Reading Stephen Dunn with Carl Dennis", and "Morning Coffee" published by *Journal of Truth and Consequence.*

"The Blooming Void: Reading *Ulysses* in Clemens Hall" published by *Elmleaves.*

"The Blind Rhetor: Dealing with the Guy Behind the TV" published by *The Writer's Compass.*

"Trying", and "Loss" published by *Tangent Literary Magazine.*

Contents

The Blooming Void

These Words

These words allow me
To step outside
The interminable flux of time
And say the things I should have said:
Render indelible
The meanings that passed ephemeral,
Like a breeze over an ocean current,
Or like the waves
Of temporarily squashed air
That got away from me,
Losing power even as they were born,
Before they could become solid, mature meaning.

These words commit me to paper,
And transubstantiate
The flesh, and the blood
And the soft, flashing orchestral arrangement
Of neural networks
That comprise this naked human's
Seat of discourse.

These words, locked in time,
And away from the wasting elements,
Away from the valley of follies and missteps
That frame my past, are a tribute,
Not just to 'should have' and 'could be'
But to the salvation of the moment:
The insustainable you and I.

Let us now find release from the tyranny of 'things'
Our own bloody pasts, unthinkable futures
And suffer out the truth
In a moment of shared silence.

The Blooming Void: Reading *Ulysses* in Clemens Hall

A lack
Of punctuation is
A sensuous airy expression

Openness

Like Molly's eight sentences
Modern man's closest glimpse at
Eternity
And natural process

She said looking out the window
Look everything is green it's spring
Spontaneous spring God's gift to man
I feel so beautiful at present

A lack of punctuation
Lends a certain ambiguity
Like the poem is the reader's
Rather than the writer's creation
Isn't it funny how the pronoun it
Can refer to a nonentity like lack
And how anything can mean everything
Or everything anything
My soul seeks connection
In disparate words phrases meanings
I want to scream in the flux
Forever adapt to the new
And therefore recognize the eternal
In each new thing

It's sexy – this undoing of punctuation
Like a void that must be filled
A vacuum
Like Molly's ethos or pathos
It reflects or refracts emotion
Understated
Like me in jeans
And in that understatement
Wrapped up like a present

This undressing of words
Impels the reader to sink into
The text
And engage in a creative act of co-authoring
The gift of creation
The most brilliant
Present

We Read with a Difference

We read with a difference
You and I.
My lens has been colored in a hue
Divergent from yours
And the thoughts we bring to each word
Create varied meaning
As we smash our opinions together
Like pin-balls
Creating new coordinates of diversity,
Perhaps
Casting light on previously unlit terrain
Or
 Synthesizing a new slant of light
On some aged topic.
And when we retire again to our repose
We can see that the light has changed
And there is another shade
That we hadn't seen before.

Mean

Meaning lives in language
And if meaning is nothing but a contrivance
Of mind
Then I'd rather live there anyways.

The mirror of words is always
A dirty gem,
A sloppy human attempt
At control and understanding –
Like every revolution:
Always born, always briefly thrashing
And always failing eventually.

But through the extremes of human
Language and thought we arrive at
A mean that works, for a time,
Until it is time
For another upheaval.

By deconstructing a bicycle
We understand its working parts
But we don't leave it, useless
Disassembled about the floor.

Likewise, language is torn apart
Cleaned inside and out
Looked at from a distance, rethought
And finally re-established in another form.

And through these flawed revolutions
And approximated binary oppositions
We find, not a reason to disperse with purpose,
But a territory for meaning and identity
A place, above all, to be.

Teaching Public School

Do you see what I see as a thirty three year old
English teacher, at a public school in the city
Whose number doesn't matter:
Aged enough to see beyond
Romance, and young enough to believe in life?
Rapture comes with the certainty and
Finality of death - the knowledge
Of defiant play: HA, I AM alive
In this eternal now, and death itself, shot dead.
This is what the students say
With laughter rather than words.
This living moment, of children who do
Not know decay, is taken as 'given.'
In my classroom we pontificate
On "Hamlet" and the implications
Of mythic Dionysus, and, yes, Mr. Cruz
The play resembles "Romeo and Juliet"
In that they die for what they believe in.

"Was he mad or just playing, Mr. Liber?"

And in the few idle moments before
The bell, the group in back with all new labels
Laughs about the kid from class/
Gunned down/ deserved it
Know who did/ shut up/ class/ punk ass/ gun you down
They holler again, not knowing that they can't,
Like a god
Put themselves back together again.

So, I'll re-create the story of my student
Who sat in the fourth row, near the wall
And had a laugh that shattered all-space
The ineluctable modality
Of the audible: pre-figuring profound
Metamorphoses in the currents of life
And the facts on the books. I'll write the
Story of the kid with the big mouth
Who didn't know boundaries, and hopefully
Heard his own expansive voice, or at least felt no pain
As he departed forever into silence.

Difference of Opinion: Reading Stephen Dunn with Carl Dennis

I have many flaws
But I do not chronicle them,
Dilate upon them, and publish them for the public
Like Stephen Dunn.

I am suffering the pangs of pragmatism in a garden of airy dreams:
Not always a romantic adventure,
That much is true.

But I have a different take on art.
Dali conceived art as "Sh*tting At light speed"
To understand my admiration, follow my logic:
Art is bequeathed from bodies -
"The world exists . . . it becomes, it passes away . . .its excrements are its food"
Art is our sustenance,
Let it be full of energy.

Stephen's voice is monotone, brown,
Imploding and taking rather than exploding and giving.

Or perhaps there is a shadow of myself
Reflected in the page
That I am too weak to acknowledge.

In Response to Sam Harris and Daniel Dennett

How holy is this science-
Hallowed in thy arts
Caress mine ears again with your refrain:
The holy chemicals in the brain.
Tell me your truth; how we expire only to be born again,
In the eyes, ears, arms, oceans of tomorrow
With nothing but that wholly gluttonous ego.
How holy is this science?

How sensuous is this science-
Hallowed in thy arts
Direct again mine wavering mind
To the proper point of reference:
Those sacred chemical compounds of bliss
So long mistaken
For nebulous love.

Dedalus

Dedalus, old artificer
It is indeed a complex labyrinth
You've built.
A shifty set of signs
Built upon the rock
Of many dead men
And much dead wood.

Stricken idol,
You are staring at me through your creation,
Trans-substantiated through this book.
Brother poet you're no ghost,
Consubstantial with your own creation,
You're real and present.

A jaded
Youth's sanctity
Crushed with sin
And misfortune
Fallen into disgrace
With the eyes of men.

You flew like eager Greek youth
Impaled yourself on failure
Rose again like a home rule sun
And in my hand I hold your body
Your blood.

But genius wills its own fall.

Metempsychosis recurs again and again -
And again how could you learn about the telephonic
Umbilical cords going back to Eve
If you hadn't closed your eyes and seen?
The cannibals and Lestrygonians are out
Will eat us all
So we may be cured of time and rotting teeth.

Soon may we walk
Through Phoenix Park
Bearing softly our ashplants
Grinning about riddles.

Forest Lawn: June 16, 1972

There was a crack on the grave
Where the water seeped in and froze
Winter after cold, ugly winter.
And I was outraged at the audacity
Of this nature
Who never knew your nature.

 I seethed with impotent rage
At things I'll never change
And wept cold, silent thoughts
That no one in this world will ever hear.

Your life is no secret and your end still a wound;
The bleeding hasn't stopped though the blood is long
dried.
A clot that generations have fought and will fight to forge
A silent war in the dominion of a few
A few that knew you;
And knew
You meant no harm.

It's a wound that can't heal
For it's a wound made of absence.
A want that can't be filled
We love you for want of your presence.

We are two strange oceans that won't ever meet
On nurturing terms that could have been
On terms that most would understand
Know,
I understand.

Long have I longed for release
And loathed my pitiful means
And envied your escaping, knowing it's not mine.
Lord knows I hope to see you at the end.

The grave casts a shadow
But shade is not enough
To shelter from the rain
Or grow new miracles.

May you rest in the peace you sought.

There was a crack on the grave
Where the water seeped in and froze
Winter after cold, ugly winter.
And I was outraged.

There was a crack on your grave
And I was outraged.

Fruit Fly in Pile of Dirty Laundry

Fruit fly in pile of dirty laundry:
From where have you arisen?
Was your antecedent in my clothes all along?
Waiting for a proper incubation?
Perhaps I was too oblivious to see your seeds waiting for
life
Or is your genesis more mystic and free?
Are you a messenger from the other side of birth?
Were you, only moments before,
A being of light looking anxious on all that is manifest?
Or have you always been just a clockwork orange:
A pile of dirt turned replicating DNA, turned survival
machine?
Fruit fly in pile of dirty laundry
From where have you arisen?

Marooned on Potomac

The school-house tower
From my window
Slices, sharp and insistent
Through its turquoise canvas
Surrounded by gradual clouds in liquid current
And sheathed in a gathering blue stream.

She shines a constant beam of the most resilient stuff
To me
On my black couch.

In her sweet unearthly peace
She sees the current
Of the lake
Run cold,
Finally freezing downstream.

Does she know that from above
She sews together this patchwork city
Of injury attorneys and bottle returns
With soft, unconditional light?

The city's pale, blind mistress in a sea of maroon.

Sludge

Sludged days in muddy-pestilent time-space.
These are the currents to crawl through,
To forget about upon passage to a spring thaw,
Buried, wheezing, but still alive.

The poetry flows like concrete,
Coagulating into a severe grip.
Thoughts are out of time
Or out of season.

Sag, rickshaw, broken window,
Frozen piss in dirty bowl,
Light bulb hangs
Out of wall,
Black duct tape its only hold
On the more stable, paint flaking wall.

In the kitchen, the apple was exhausted:
Brown, imploded, growing other organisms -
Submitting to entropy and becoming useful
On some micro-level.

The fruit bowl turned into an indeterminate
Brown sludge
That she said would work well
As fertilizer.

The Moon

Your light shone off
Shards of broken glass,
Sharp
Sinking deep, insistent
Dissolving inside my flesh.

The street,
A silvery ocean
With thin skin
Reflecting
The depths
Of your sea.

Tiny ripples
Surface,
Shake my center.
I shiver
Like a blade of grass
On a shifting beach
Under a renewed you.

It happens:
When you give a crooked smile – quizzical but tempted,
And you cock your head slightly to the side
And your make-up is running
And you're surprised enough to laugh
And shaken enough to be stirred
And you shine through
Through all the turbulence and fanfare
And your watery essence
Is palpable
In an unguarded moment.
There is a wise sadness in your smile
I could live there forever.
Enveloped in this warm bath
Renewed and renewing
I see new dawn in your eyes.

The Old Water

Behold the old water!
It abounds with steely life!
Long left to grow
In purple-plastic cup
In the tepid sink,
Rich
With residues of celebration
A swirling tempest of spirit and soul.

Behold the old water!
Seething with the miracles of birth
For each hearty organism
In your mysterious depths
A thousand worlds remain unseen.

Behold the old water!
Who am I to disturb you?
Ah, but a foolish human upset your grace, fair pool.

The Sky is Full of Blues

The sky is full of blues
Swirling low
On such a moody day.
The music wafting from the neighbor's
Has an amethystine glow
That sparks a light sadness
In this searing, frozen moment.
The moon is out at noon
Brighter than the sun
Awakening me to
Last night's radiance.
And on the bed next to me
A stranger
In runny make up
Sleeping displaced
From usual arrangements,
Curling next to me
Giving my soul
A horrible thrill
On such a moody day,
Swirling low,
The sky is full of blues.

Yellow Warbler

Yellow warbler
With coat so fine
Each bristle
Trembling with each push
Of wind

Flailing
Hither and Thither
Gaining a full
Zero
Of direction

But still seeming
To smile through the
Pushes
How I am like you
Yellow warbler

Bluing

Bluing isn't becoming
Of you darling

In gardens of yes
Your heart grows red

I shiver with heat
Watching the sea-dog simmer

And eyes bloom
Some new species of rainbow

Fiery Green

She wore a fiery green dress
And her eyes, all ablaze
Sunk savage hooks in my rapt flesh.
The world all around
Budded on the 6th of May:
Fluttered white, pink, emerald.

Dusty sarcophagus mind
Had no where to hide.
The rotten, swollen sores
Were getting such sweet air
Even the seething boils
Of recent philosophy turned their essences
Heavenward.

She wore a fiery green dress
And spread a fierce healing
That moves me
Even today
In less inspired
Moments.

I Awoke with a Start

I awoke with a start -
From the ether into little, burgeoning body;
Out of the stars and wind into a sea-sick body,
Gaining equilibrium,
Looking out on the falling leaves.

I awoke with a start in a warm nest,
And presently plunged tender foot
Unto frozen, ice-cube floor
Shuddering momentarily and
Setting out from my bedroom
On the farm.

By the stairs was a bookshelf,
All books I'd never read.
I gleaned at them with ravenous thoughts,
Looking at Tolstoy, *Learning Russian* and Edgar Cayce,
And proceeded down the stairs
Where were the adults
Who had risen
Before I.

And in the dining room
Staring through a crystal punch bowl
Time ceased and dissolved.
As I listened to the voices
Of the noble veterans of
Of the material world:
Nana, Papa, Dad and Mom,
I felt them as they are
Out of time,
Not bound the craggy
And transient
Samsara world,
I wanted to tell them
It would all be OK.
But I hardly had the vocabulary.

I was new here.
Not blinded by dirt.
I wanted so badly to tell them
It would all be OK.
And before I actually went
And hugged and kissed
I heard, for the first time, about cancer.

Look Forward

Look forward
For the past is a weighty anchor
Whose heavy contemplation
Brings the solitude of hobgoblins.
This chain,
Though it feels cold and stern,
Is a child's closet.
It is funny,
This shackle that feels so real
Has only the gravity of dreams.

Look around you.
Where does it lie, this past?
Only the present carries the mass and inertia
Of now.

Look forward
For we know the center doesn't hold
And even as this axis slips away
We must find a foothold in the new.

Open, empirical eyes
And do as you must
Look forward.

Melody so Slow

Melody so slow
Wrap your arms around me
Curl around woody bass,
Breathy and voiced
With fat lips.

Careening sly about the thrush
Coy and oily
Smooth shocks over
Pulsing waves
Undulating all around
The expected line.

Teasing and touching
The anticipated thrust
Bringing the whole pulse to an intolerable surge
Coming to your own peak
Outside the fleshy
Rhythm
Whispering truth and beauty
Into my open ear.

Morning Coffee

Wisdom is a symptom of bleeding hearts
Served cold over shaking, rattling coffee cups.
The walls are bright
Screaming with the memories they've seen.
My eyes are glossed and stinging.
We huddle close
As if the only surviving victims of some unseen war.
The new sun comes purple and frozen into the restaurant.

Morning Light

At some point -
Everyone feels the weight of their decisions,
Their own free-will.

More than anything
The past looks back at me now
Like a pale, sullen ghost
A valley of follies and missteps
Of mistakes and wrong directions,
But still I find solace
In one move:

Watching you through streaks of morning light
Sleeping by my side
Soft and satisfied.

My Hands

"My hands are so cold
They're burning"
She said walking into our house.

My dear, I too have gone so
Far at times that
Night turns to day
And all the sensuous enticement
Turned to bitter dissolute, hollow.

I've lived in the world where I could
Smell green
All day
Until I could
Feel the orange burn of the sunset
Turn my stomach
Towards dinner
And I could put away
My big wheel
Happy that I'd played all day long.
And now my playmate's got
Three kids
And a teaching job
And all changes.

May all
That we think well today
Not deceive us and turn
Malignant tomorrow
May all morphology be, in the end, benevolent.

"Do you want a cup of tea?"
She asked, unpacking the groceries.

We Two

We two see the same rain
And have known an ocean of troubles,
Usurping the sky and eclipsing the sun
Metamorphosing once brilliant heavens
Changing the horizon to indeterminate concrete
Overtaking the kingdom of thought and free breath
Looming over all the living and all the dead.
We see the rain, feel it slither down our skin
Assailed by the same titanic cloud
On different sides of the city.
We both let the rain bleed down deep
And through it, I feel your warm blood
Beyond, but with me
And like the poet who sang of spring
In spontaneous prose
I keep a piece of your soul
Locked in my soul
For all time -
From the time beyond time
Where my soul may rest with yours in ancient peace.
I am not bashful or timid like the sky.
I will not be usurped.
I will hold that piece of your soul with distinguished
violence
Locked in my everliving heart
And will clash with the fevered mass
Holding my ground with your soul inside me, burning
bright.
A sea of idiots in an over flown world could never
overtake me;
None hold the key.
We two see the same rain.
May it not taint your eyes with slow decay
But let it be an agent of budding growth and change
My child of May.

Wet Soul

I have a slightly wet soul
That presents herself
In washed-out moments between
Sleep, dream, and waking
When all time's egg cracks open
And the yolk of the everlasting
Is viscous, palpable.

She bares herself
When children's cries,
Ringing through the early March
Faded dark wine dusk,
Reverberate off
My awakening bedroom walls
I can feel the
Mounds of melting brown snow
In their cries:
Earth, us, them, I,
All part of the same ripple.

She shows herself
When all the world is awaking
From a cold and sodden winter
And the tungsten of pure being
Shimmers with frail waves of
Transience.

There is a placid peace
In her pools of soft wisdom
And I know
That the child is the father
Of the man
Though I can see little reason
In leaving amniotic waters.

I remember, then, why
Fragile ideas like emotion and faith
Made sense once
And forget why
They were swept under the carpet of
Uselessness
In favor of hard truth
And remember why
Silly things like compassion
Are important.

I have a wet soul
That still comes out of hiding
In rare moments.

With Friend

With friend
Said Holly Bear
The green is greener
And day more happy
Even night
Is
Good
Those stars
Shine real bright in their
Big moon pie
When I'm
With friend

Zero

It all adds up to a great big -
Balancing act.

Piecing together the shards
Of a puzzle without end or beginning
Slipping in and out of meaning
Chasing a prime cause
Or primal, sexy apocalypse.

Staring at lights from the twenty eighth floor
Primordial, intelligent chaos
A speck of drywall on my finger
Easily crushed
Turned to dust
And then dirty air.

Cabs cry in chilled air
Spilling demons
To the walls of facades
Who don't want to hear.
Icy vapors float in vermillion sky,
Free in their abandon.
The cloud of chaos
Flowing in eternal patterned dance
The whole - trying to understand itself
Through a dissipated parallax
Getting a grip occasionally
And seeking beyond all things
To find a measure of
Balance,
Trying to go back home
Where it all
Began.

Befriend Your Demons

Befriend your demons
Because they are with you for a lifetime.
Though the pieces you are today
Aren't the pieces you were,
Entelechy, master of form
Sees through entropy.

The curs at your heels
Are uniquely yours.
Feed them, they are hungry.
Like all that lives and decays
And feeds off all else
Exchanging molecules,
Body fluids
And ideas
Feed the mutt of metempsychosis:
It is your responsibility.

Be polite
Because 'demon' is a relative term
And the trap jaw on your ankle
Is someone else's child.

Be polite -
Because your demons
Unbeknownst to you
Are really Heaven sent:
Products of good conscience,
Or perhaps an ill-advised bad conscience;
Be careful delineating -
Because, as the German philosophers
Have writ, there's a difference.

Befriend your demons
For they are your children.

Bikinis are Out

Bikinis are out
The 1st of the year.
At this pace
Plastic Santas will be staring into a hot July dusk soon
Looking for an owner
Not knowing
Where the hell they are.

At this pace
We'll lap the calendar backwards
And Christmas trees will be on sale in January
For the next year.
And the fashion year will be
More than a year ahead of the calendar
Or behind –
Depending on perspective.

And if that trend still continues
We'll lap ourselves again
And there will come a year
When bikinis are out
Some time in October '16
For the summer of '18
And all the executives will look at each other
And say
"What the hell is wrong? Why is nothing selling?"

And somewhere
Reason will smile.

Late Capitalism

It's too bad
We can't talk about
Late Capitalism
The same way
We talk about
My Great Grand-father Samuel
Who was a great man
And served the community
And retired happily
To a man more fit for his position
To watch a new generation
Grow up around him
And died softly one night;
No one really noticing
When he passed out of this world.
We all keep his memory
Like a wreath of maple leaves
Fondly in our hearts.

Looking; Or the Transcendent Polemic

Looking for a transcendent politics
And politicians who live on
Their future reputations as
The great remembered:
Sensitive politicians who grow into their roles
As the lochs and gatekeepers of mankind,
As innocent and naturally,
As the fruits of September.
We are looking for spirits strong enough
To weather storms of dissent and polemics;
To hold off the horses of a hot, lusty night
For the benefit of a million grateful descendants.
We are looking for spirits strengthened by the slashing
rains,
Holding fast like the oak,
And wise enough to remember when oaths
Had the power to bend men's will.
We are all open and eager now
For the few
Who can suspend basic greed
For the sake of children.
In thinking of all but yourself –
Hypothetical leader,
You've raised yourself above us all
And make yours an estate
Not of this coarse world,
But in the hearts and minds,
The true fruit,
Of all those you unchained.

Lord of the Land

Fair and Just
Lord of the land
Batter my heart with your three pronged Justice:
I will live without that thermostat;
Show me the resilience sleeping comfortably within me;
Beat out of me the strength I never knew I had;
I will render unto you the fees that are yours;
I've taken my vow and my tithe;
Your rise in rent is just and necessary;
I will render unto you what is yours;
The leak in the roof will teach me tolerance and
How to appreciate the ceiling over my head
Fair and Just
Lord of the Land
Batter my heart with your three pronged Justice.

Normal Street

Police Sirens bring me to the window
Like the rest of the neighborhood
This Thursday morning.

Everyone looking for meaning
In a shrill wail that unites us in an urgent moment
Allowing our thoughts to congeal -
"What happened?"

It's the pain that brings us together
Humanity can always fall back on destruction
For a sense of immediacy.

The lights
Reflect off broken windows,
Jagged edges,
Fragmented glass,
And glitter,
Not unlike a carnival.

No wonder we mistake.

Police sirens bring me to the window
Like the rest of the neighborhood
This Thursday morning.

The New Slavery

The new slavery
Comes to us as toys under the tree
With little marks that read
Made in China.

The new slavery
Sweats 15 hours a day
With a pittance for a wage
And somber resignation.

The new slavery
Is written into the frowning hide
Of honest men and women of all nations under the sun
Fighting for the means to survive.

The new slavery
Is smiled on from warm shadows
By the current administration
And blessed by their God.

The corporate oligarchy, Exxon
Gave Lee Raymond in 2005
$144,000 a day / $6,000 an hour.
Blessed be.

They gave Lee a $400,000,000 retirement parachute
For which to sail down softly
And crush the backs of poor working fools
Under polished black leather boots.

The new slavery
Is written into the souls of Americans
Who can't find a job
That's moved overseas.

The new slavery comes down
As sweet little toys under Christmas trees.

Thirty Years' Children

Thirty years' children
Who have lived without knowing how.
Subject to such wanton and wild slips
As are companion to
Youth and liberty,
Groping for solid ground
In an ever shifting
Charybdis.

Sucking down and around
Cold waters
Exploding brains
With
Useless information.

Trying to reconcile
Past parties
That gave us identity
With
Present day.

Trying to reconcile the truth
That we are next
On the ferris wheel of creation
To taste what's underground
After creating new life
Out of nothing:
A miracle.

Trying

Try as you might to extinguish my blood
It sings and dances at your approach.
And things held to my eye as brutal inequality
Are reasons to leap above matter and
Sink sincere impulse into a crying lot:
Shard organized silence and
Break nothing but the bars of 'no real learning.'

From where have we dreamt this violent peace?
This armored Eden?
This ocean of Cheshire eyes singing with gleeful shrugs?
This grid of aging babies tied to
Electric guide posts riveted to the reptilian brain?
This Trojan advance of overfed cyborg children
Who don't know the difference between
An adjective and an adverb or
A noun and a reason for being?
Steeped in self love, our cup is long
Overflown and my drowning cries
Are much stronger and more musical
Than anything I could have dreamt of
Prior.

Let grow
The forests of the mind upon which
Theories thrive and the power of stately death
Is killed
Dead,
Where the direction of "What?" turns right
And the compass bears all
Returning to omnidirectional love in a
Direct and precise
Moment.

Try as you might to extinguish my blood
I sing and dance
At your approach.

War

There's a war on the middle class
And we're none too quick
To admit
We're the ones drowning;
Because hope is far too strong
A stimulant
And optimism
Far too strong a sedative,

Ignorance
Far too great a pleasure
And a thorny truth
Much too easy to ignore.

Good and Evil
Have dissolved into a viscous mess
That there's really no way to separate
Other than with inhuman patience.

There's a war on the middle class
And we're none too quick to admit it.

Gravity and Impulse

It all runs on gravity and impulse.
The things that we did today in class
Were things I'd been walked through
As a student, scripts that had been seared into
My head, before I understood the world through
The cold calculus of dirty logic.

Peeling myself off the chair in my office
Was no easy feat, but I was urged by
The invisible hand of power or responsibility.
By 8:01 I was a dirty faced boy playing hooky.
Walking into class at 8:03
I had no plan, a few vague words and memories
Of past classes. I wrote the pre-fix "meta" on
The board, and, of course, I ended up giving you
The answer after I posed the question – "How does this
Change the meaning of a word?"
You all grasped at straws, and I found myself equally
Awkward in my explanation: "It indicates a concept
Which is an abstraction from another concept"
And then we all learned a little
About metaphors and metacognition,
Mostly spewing platitudes:
"A comparison using 'like' or 'as'."
And no wonder this world has become
A capital producing work camp for the already-bloated:
The workers or becoming-workers are all given dry,
understandable orders,
Told to perform some inconsequential task,
Then sent to the next
Station with bells and whistles,
Prodded along by bigger animals
In suits. The game looks official,
But it's mindless, forgettable, especially
When we can strap on an iPod or graft ourselves to hope
Streaming through a TV screen: brilliant anesthesia.
What happened to this world – a stage?
All order of difference and development
Brimming over in spontaneous overflow?

It's not your fault class. The enemy is safe behind
Invisible stockades of false logic and polluted hope.
Your mission, now, is to leap above impulse
And the urge to agree, and ferret out the cold steel
Of coercion from the promise of all your desires.
Defy the natural gravity, cut the cancer out of
Your own heart, and dare to feel
The gravity of your own voice.

The Blind Rhetor

The blind rhetor wields rosebud-artillery
From behind the broad cast front lines:
Shells filled with fish-hooks
Designed to catch the handles of your eyes.

And though the blind night has imposed
A flailing protocol
The extinction of eyesight and proximity
Increases the sense of audience-invoked.

The spongy gropings and intuitions
Of the sightless aggressor
Gain precision
With time.

This soft war in the dominion
Of all with wide, sanguine eyes
Is waged on the front of the reptilian brain
Quiet, imperceptible, like arsenic.

Or like rain that falls through cracks
In the roof, freezing with the night
All pathology is left silent
For your shadow to hide.

Until, like paradox, the inside turns out,
Looks at itself, tries to match the images
And, failing, tries to carry on:
A barrier between real and "I."

Loss

Behind the handles of your eyes
Are the strings of your mind
And before there even was an "I"
They've been tugging at you from behind
TV billboards – a soft campaign
Sinking light persuasion deep -
Until there is a confusion about
What is and isn't "I."

You saw fear and loathing,
Read Kerouac,
Grafted your soul to the anti-hero,
Despised authority,
And for all that I can't blame you
But, what I'm most sorry about
Is your blindness to the lack of solutions.
What you've sought is a blissful death
And if you don't unglaze your eyes
You'll soon find half of that equation.

I was walking through the living autumn
On Veteran's day, when everyone else was at the mall
And saw, scrawled unsubstantial on stone:
"Live every day like it's your last"
And I thought, what a stupid idea
Born of ignorance and impatience.
And then I hesitated –
I would've reveled in that foolish advice ten years gone
And then I thought of you sitting in my class
More like a looking-glass,
Spouting anti-authoritarian slogans,
Trying to organize an academic coup,
Throwing your hands up at politics.
And it was like a mirror on classes past
Betraying the seeds
Of your hypothetical future dissertation.

Then I looked at the swaying trees
All things pass.
As I walked back to my car I scribbled these lines:

If tragedy is born from wasted potential
Then we've got a holocaust of goodwill
In the middle of a heaving nation

What Words

What words
Can do
Is move
The flood
In the
Right directions
For fertile
Fields to
Grow on
Stalks of
Rhetoric aimed
At creating
A better world:
Peace, love.
Can you
Believe it?

Peter Fernbach, Assistant Professor of English at Adirondack Community College, is concerned, lately, with the transformative and liberating effects of poetry on the unconscious mind, especially of those who are still impressionable and exploding with exuberance and possibility. He thinks that poetry, as an art, and also as an epistemological approach, is undervalued in our increasingly semiotic culture; the ways of knowing that are provided by and through poesis are progressively being choked out in favor of a simplistic empiricism that allows for none of the nuance of the mystifying reality of which we are all a part. Therefore, most of all, he invites you to read.